FAIRLY ODD JOKES

Based on the TV show *The Fairly OddParents™* created by Butch Hartman as seen on Nickelodeon®

ISBN 0-439-62343-X

12 11 10 9 8 7 6 5 4 3 2 1   04/11   4 5 6 7 8/0

Printed in the U.S.A.

First Scholastic printing, January 2004

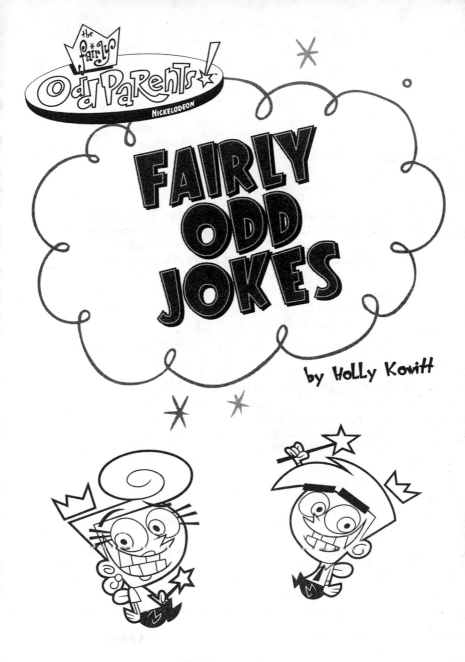

FAIRLY ODD JOKES

by Holly Kowitt

SCHOLASTIC INC.

New York   Toronto   London   Auckland   Sydney
Mexico City   New Delhi   Hong Kong   Buenos Aires

TABLE OF CONTENTS

Who's the Fairiest of Them All? 5

One Good Turner Deserves Another 18

Totally Jaw-some 25

Spaced Out 34

Torturing Timmy Turner 37

Fairly Odd Friends 42

Poof! Poof! Who's There? 46

WHO'S THE FAIRIEST OF THEM ALL?

What's the best thing about being a fairy?
Frequent flyer miles.

Why did Cosmo and Wanda get a vacuum cleaner?
Because the house was full of fairy dust.

What kind of fish are Cosmo and Wanda?
Flying fish!

What do you call someone who can turn herself into a werewolf with the wave of her wand?
A hairy godmother.

POOF!

What do you call someone who grants wishes and goes "Moo, moo"?
A dairy godmother.

POOF!

What's Cosmo's favorite
amusement park ride?
The fairy-go-round.

Why would Cosmo and Wanda
make good balloons?
Because there's air in every fairy.

Which state has the
most fairies?
Wish-consin.

Why did Cosmo dye the
Easter Bunny green?
Because he really likes
green hare.

What do fairies catch a lot
of when they play baseball?
Fly balls.

Why did Wanda change
Cosmo into a clock?
She wanted to see time
fly.

Why does Jorgen von Strangle like visiting the dentist? Because he knows all the drills.

What cheese do they serve at the Fairy Academy? Jorgen-zola!

Who has the largest furniture in Fairy World? Jorgen—he's got a big chest!

POP!

What seafood does
Jorgen like best?
Mussels.

What kind of stories
does Jorgen tell?
Tall tales.

Who grants wishes to young fishermen?
Fairy CodParents.

What do all fairy movies have?
A zappy ending.

Why couldn't the lawyer win a case in Fairy Court?
He didn't have any poof!

When Cosmo turns into a
dog, what does he wag?
His fairy tail.

POOF!

What do you call Timmy's godmother when she turns into a superhero?
Wanda Woman.

How do fairies improve their TV reception?
With a satellite wish.

ONE GOOD TURNER DESERVES ANOTHER

Why did Timmy lose friends when he became invisible? Everyone could see right through him.

What does a wand do at a football game? The wave.

Why do fairies go to the dentist?
To get their teeth crowned.

What do you have when Cosmo and
Wanda wear mink coats?
Furry GodParents.

Who grants wishes to young
trumpets?
The Toot Fairy.

What do you get when Wanda zaps cars to match Timmy's hat? A pink car-nation.

How do you catch a fairy? By the fairy tale.

What sign hangs in all of the restaurant bathrooms in Fairy World? *"Employees Must Wash Wings Before Returning to Work"*

Why did Cleft, the Boy Chin Wonder, fight the Bronze Kneecap and Spatula Woman? Because they kept trying to break the jaw.

What happened to the Boy Chin Wonder when the Crimson Chin ran on ahead? He was Cleft behind.

What is the Chin's favorite kind of cookie? Crimson Chip.

spaced out

How do you learn to
be a space hero?
Take a Crash course.

What does Crash
Nebula call a
killer potato?
His starch-enemy.

What do you get when a killer
potato stomps on Timmy's
favorite space hero?
Mash Nebula.

What did Mark, the alien prince, say to the book? "Take me to your reader!"

What does Mark, the alien prince, watch every year on TV? *The Out-of-This-World Series.*

Why did Vicky hand Timmy over to the school bullies? She wanted everyone to have a Turner.

TORTURING TIMMY TURNER

Timmy: "Why'd you tell everyone that I'm a twerp?"
Vicky: "I didn't know it was supposed to be a secret!"

What's Vicky's favorite day of the week?
Mean-day.

What is Vicky's favorite book?
How to Get Rich Baby-sitting by
Robin D. Turners.

What did Timmy yell to his mom when
Vicky called?
"The phony's for you."

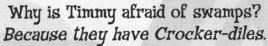
Why is Timmy afraid of swamps?
Because they have Crocker-diles.

What is Timmy's
teacher's favorite snack?
Cheese and Crockers.

Why does Timmy have
to watch out for Mr.
Crocker?
He's fairy suspicious!

What do you call a
fairy-hunting squid?
A Crock-topus.

FAIRLY ODD FRIENDS

Why doesn't A.J. spend any money?
He's saving for a brainy day.

What does Timmy's scout
leader order with his
hamburger?
Squirrelly fries.

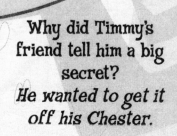

Why did Timmy's
friend tell him a big
secret?
*He wanted to get it
off his Chester.*

What kind of underwear
does Chet Ubetcha wear?
News briefs!

Why did Chet take a
job on a ship?
He wanted to be an
anchor man.

What happened when Chet
broke his leg?
He ended up in a news cast.

POOF! POOF! WHO'S THERE?

Knock-knock.
Who's there?
Cosmo.
Cosmo who?
You Cosmo trouble than
any fairy I know!

Knock-knock.
Who's there?
Wanda.
Wanda who?
Wanda where Timmy went.